What to doodle?

AMAZING ANIMALS!

Chuck Whelon

DOVER PUBLICATIONS, INC.
Mineola, New York

Doodling is so much fun—just grab a pencil and see where your imagination takes you! We've made it easy to enjoy doodling in this unique book—just add your own ideas to the sixty-two exciting picture pages. For example, you can draw the contents of a hungry whale's stomach, as well as teeth for a crocodile, antlers for a moose, and a rider for a camel. You'll find many more amazing animals, too, such as a boa constrictor, a silverback gorilla, and even a jerboa. Let's get started!

Bibliographical Note

What to Doodle? Amazing Animals! is a new work, first published by
Dover Publications, Inc., in 2009.

International Standard Book Number

ISBN-13: 978-0-486-47266-9
ISBN-10: 0-486-47266-3

Manufactured in the United States by RR Donnelley
47266305   2016
www.doverpublications.com

What is this elephant carrying on its back?
Have fun finishing the picture!

Now decorate the wings of this delightful creature.

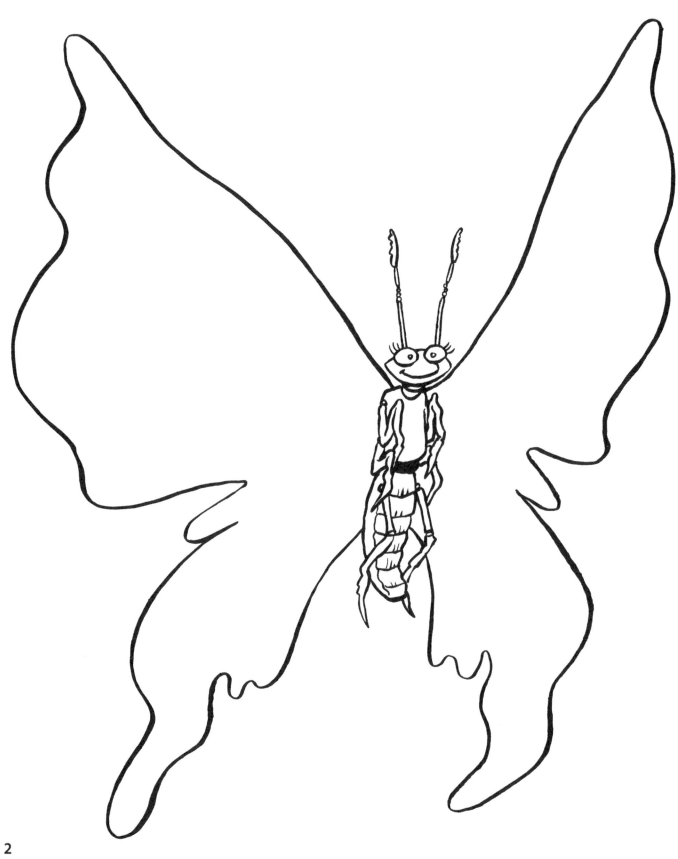

What do you think this boa constrictor has trapped? Draw a picture of it.

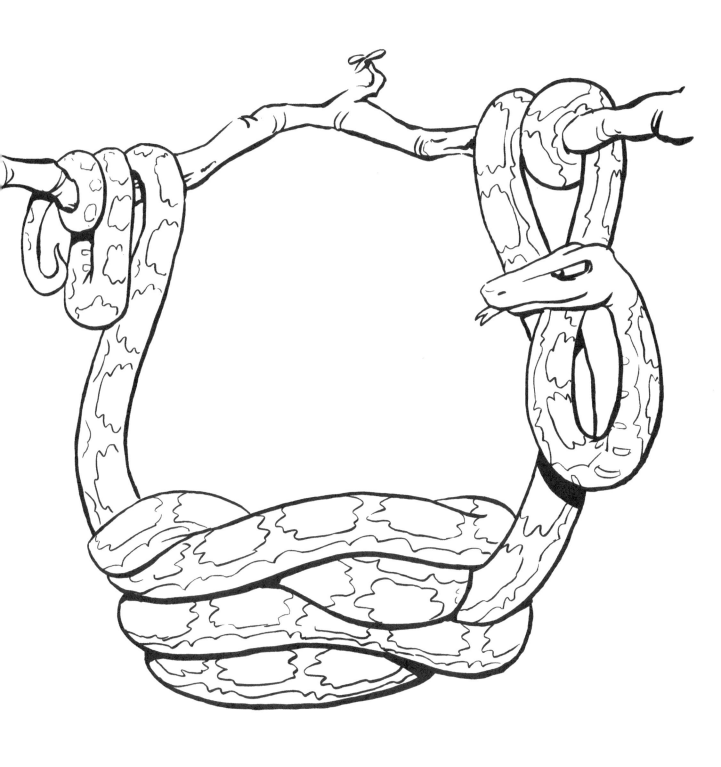

Draw a picture of the large silverback gorilla that is the leader of this troop.

What has made this charging rhinoceros so angry? Draw its picture.

Draw an animal that is even odder-looking than this warthog.

Giraffes use their long necks to gather food.
Draw a picture of what you think this giraffe is eating.

Everyone knows that the lion is the king of beasts.
Draw a few of the animals in his kingdom.

This dolphin is carrying a camera for the U.S. Navy Marine Mammal Program. Draw a picture of what the dolphin will photograph.

This dog works for a police department.
Draw a picture of what it has found.

The tiny hummingbird is feeding from a flower. Draw its picture.

What have these rascally raccoons discovered in the trash? Draw it!

Can you draw a picture of some things
that this enormous whale has swallowed?

What does this kangaroo have in her pouch? Draw what it looks like.

Draw a picture of a friend for this lonely platypus.

These tourists are being watched by an animal in the tree.
Draw a picture to show what it looks like.

A horse is gracefully jumping over the fence. Draw its picture.

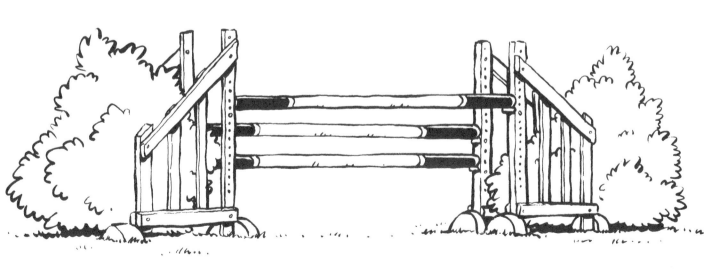

Draw a picture of the dog team that is pulling the sled through the blizzard.

**What's a zebra without its stripes?
Draw some on this confused animal!**

What have the monkeys taken from the researcher?
Finish the picture any way you wish.

This camel is in a hurry. Draw a picture of its frightened rider.

What do you think is going on inside
this gigantic termite mound? Draw it.

This chameleon can blend into its surroundings.
Draw what it is hiding in.

This frog is catching something with its tongue.
Guess what it might be and finish the picture.

Draw the tiny animals that can be seen through the powerful microscope.

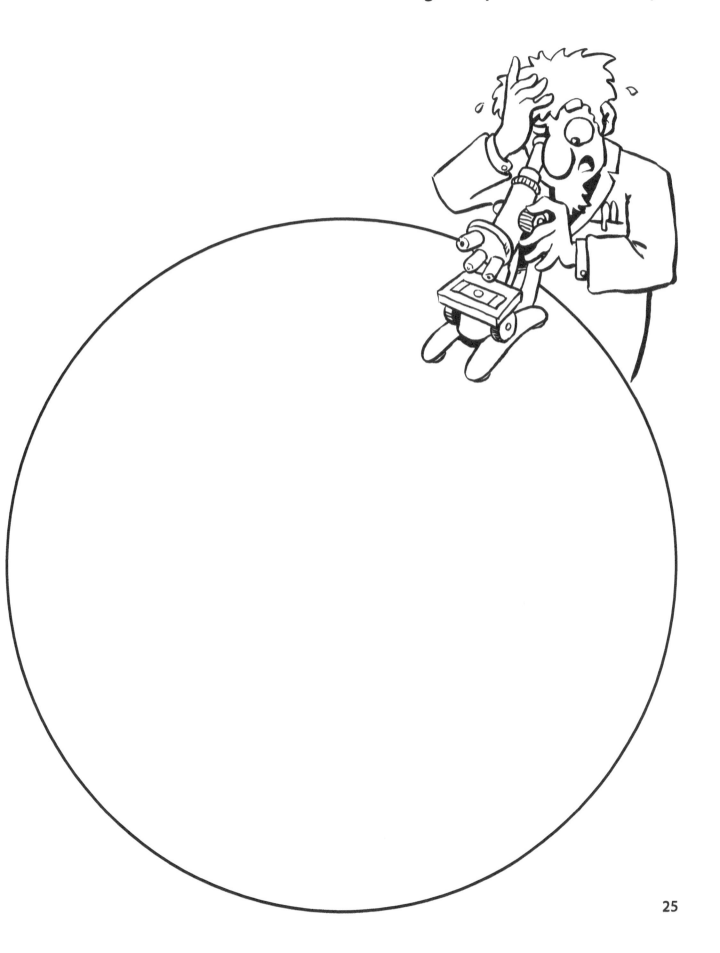

A ferocious animal is chasing this hunter.
Show what it looks like.

Daisy has a number of unusual animals on her farm.
Draw a picture of a few of them.

Draw the amazing new animal that these scientists have discovered.

If you could save an animal from extinction,
what would it be? Draw its picture.

Draw a pair of majestic antlers on this moose.

How would you ride an ostrich? Draw it!

Fill out this crocodile's smile with some teeth.

Draw the sea creature that this boy is riding on.

This crab is missing its pincers. You can help by drawing them.

This giant tortoise on the Galapagos Islands is more than one hundred years old. Can you draw its grandmother?

Draw some animals that you might find in the frozen Arctic region.

What is this snow leopard creeping up on? Draw its picture.

Draw a picture of some lucky animals that have found this tasty picnic lunch.

Add some details to the picture to show where this badger lives.

Something has surprised these meerkats—show what it is.

Draw a picture of the animals that these hunters are waiting for.

This cheetah is racing after something. Draw it.

If you could design a national flag, what animal would you pick for it? Draw it here.

Draw the spider that has spun this enormous web.

Oh, no! Belinda has spotted a creature crawling up her back! Draw its picture—and hurry!

What exotic animal would you like as a pet? Draw it right here.

Create some markings for this strange lizard.

What is this little jerboa hopping away from? Finish the picture.

Draw the animals that live in this burrow.

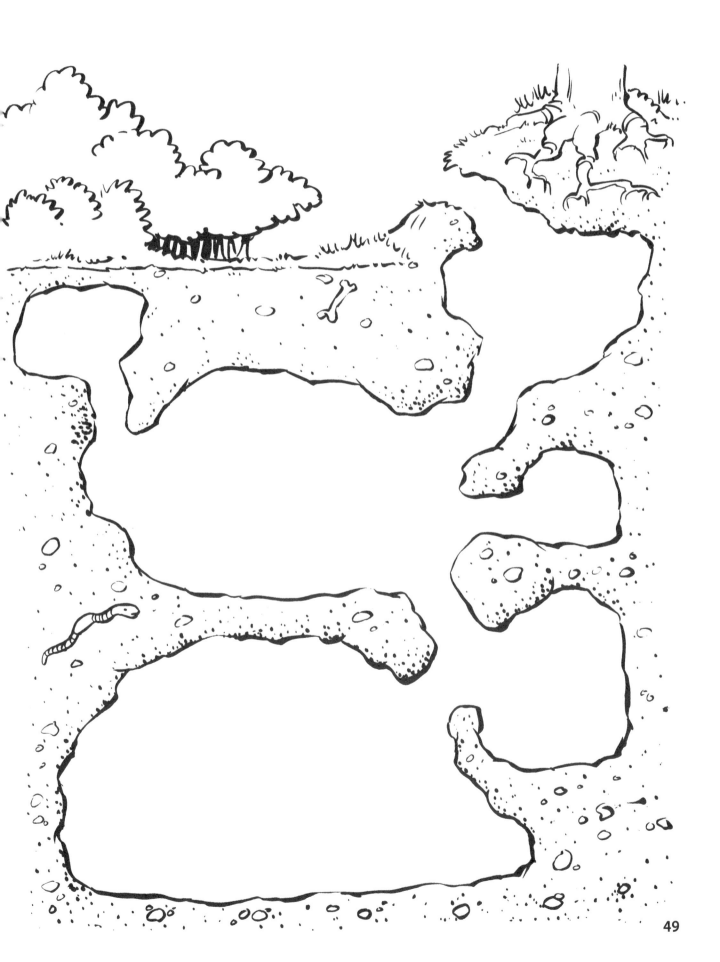

Now draw a nice, long, striped tail for this lemur.

**What has hatched out of these eggs?
It's up to you to complete the picture.**

Draw a picture of the orangutan that lives in the nest.

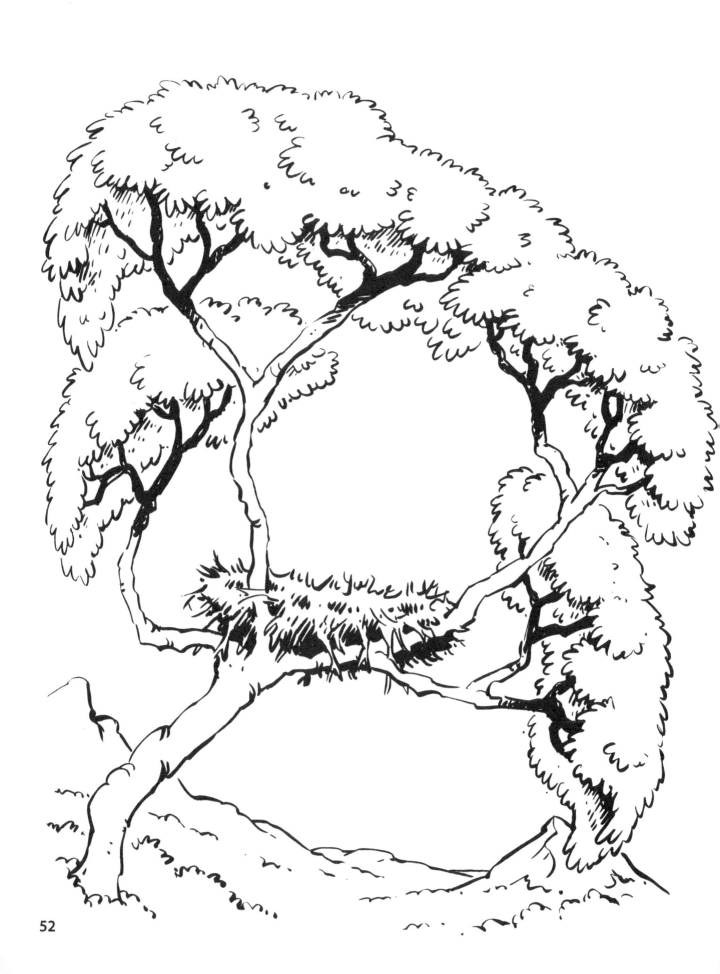

Draw the animals that live beneath the surface of this African river.

Add to the picture the beavers that worked so hard to build this dam.

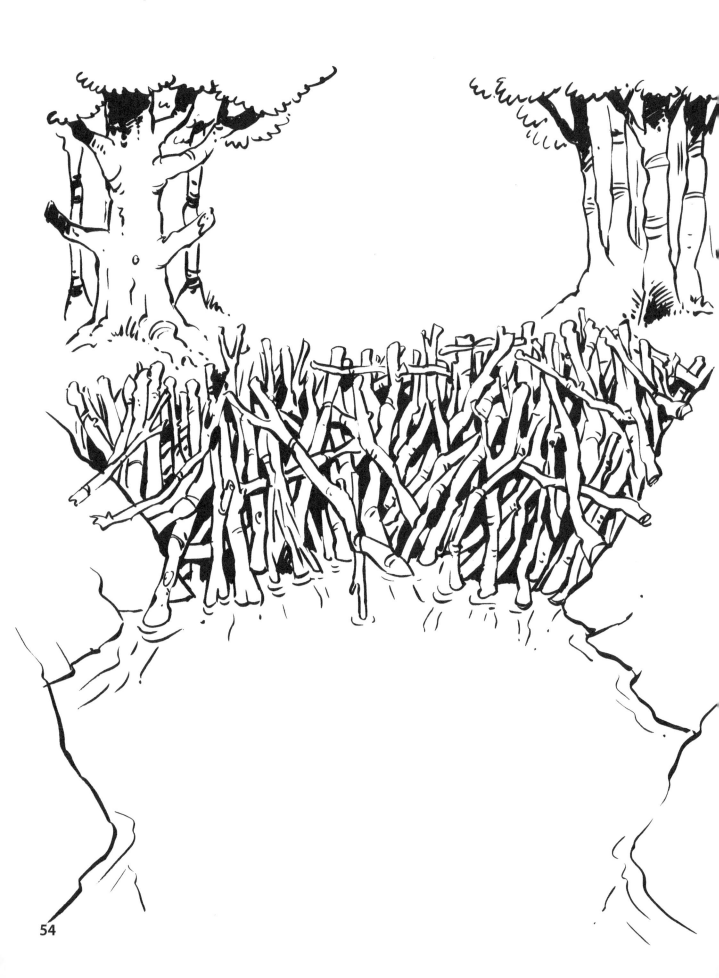

Add some details to the picture and then see how
colorful you can make this parrot's plumage.

Draw a picture of the animal that belongs to this shell.

This tide pool is full of creatures—draw some of them.

This tiger is relaxing with its cubs. Add them to the picture.

Fill this page with flamingos to keep Pinky company.

Many colorful fish live around this coral reef. Show what they look like.

Can you guess what is chasing this jackrabbit? Draw it!

Draw a picture of the panda that lives in this bamboo forest.